My 26 Week
Gratitude Journal

ISBN: 978-1-949474-92-3
Edition: May 2020

For all inquiries, please contact us at:
info@puppysmiles.org

To see more of our books, visit us at:
www.PuppyDogsAndIceCream.com

D1279196

Message Just For You...

We know how fun you are so we have included lots of really cool games and activities for you and your buddy.

P.S. Hope you love the stickers inside!

Sending you lots of Positive Vibes

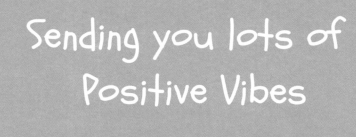

Positive Vibes

Note to Parent

Gratitude is about focusing on the good and being thankful
for the things we have in our life.
The purpose of this 26 week journal is to establish simple weekly
fun acts of gratitude which positively impact a child's development.

Scientific benefits include:

Increases Happiness & Wellbeing
Increases Self-Esteem & Confidence
Encourages a Growth Mindset
Improves Relationships at home & school
Builds Resilience & a positive outlook

How to use the Journal

This journal consists of weekly fun activities & games.
Each weekly acitivity can be removed from the journal and put in
a place for the child to see daily.
For eg. on the fridge/in their bedroom

It is important that the child is encouraged to do the activities on
a weekly basis and parents get involved to make it a fun
family exercise.

This Journal belongs to:

Name _____

&

My Journal Buddy is:

*A Buddy can be a Parent, Friend or close Relative

Name _____

Stick a photo or draw picture below!

Me

My buddy

What is Gratitude?

Gratitude = Give Thanks

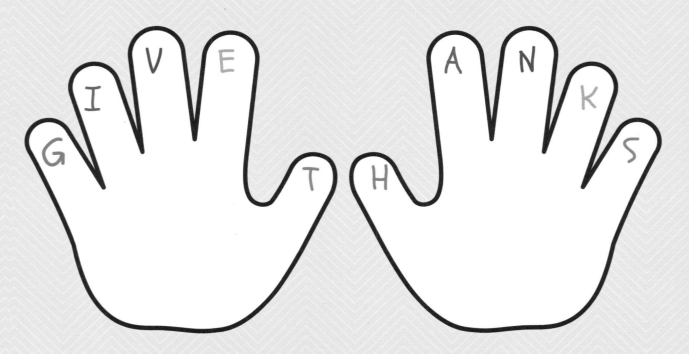

G ratitude	**T** hank everyone
I s	**H** elp everyone
V ery	**A** ppreciate all you have
E asy	**N** otice all the good things in life
	K now your talents
	S erve others

All About Me!

My name is _____

I am ___ years old

My favourite colour is _____

My best friend is _____

My favourite book is

_____

My favourite food is

_____

My favourite place is

_____

I am thankful for...

Colour in all your favourite things that you are thankful for below. Think about why they make you happy.

Toys to play with

My Family

Sunshine

Clothes to wear

ME

Flowers

My home

My friends

Colouring

Food to eat

Week 2

5 Things
I love about myself..

Write 5 things you love about yourself (see examples below). Try saying them every night this week before bed!

1. I am_____

2. I am_____

3. I am_____

4. I am_____

5. I am_____

KIND

HEALTHY

HAPPY

SPECIAL

BRAVE

CLEVER

Best Buddies Handprint

Trace and colour in your handprint below.
On all five fingers write one thing you like
about each other!

Week 4

kind

funny

Buddy
hand print

strong

cool

My hand
print

This week includes two activities,
check out the next page!

Gratitude Name Game

 Name a person that makes you smile

 Name a place that makes you happy

 Name your favourite food

 Name a friend that makes you giggle

 Name one thing that you like about yourself

How to play?

Ask your buddy to pick a colour –
Pink or Red or Yellow or Green or Blue

Whatever colour they pick ask them the question
next to it.
Remember to take turns!

Week 4

My Family Tree

Stick or draw pictures of your family on the leaves of your Family Tree above!

What I love about my body

1. _____

2. _____

3. _____

What is special about me

1. _____

2. _____

3. _____

Draw a
picture of
yourself
here

Week 6

What my body does for me

1. _____

2. _____

3. _____

How can I keep myself
strong & healthy

1. _____

2. _____

3. _____

Mindful Colouring

What are your favourite colours?
Get crayons, markers, or colouring
pencils and colour in the picture below!

This week includes two activities,
check out the next page!

Gratitude Yoga Poses

🎵 Play your favourite music

I am strong like a tree

Pretend to be a Tree
A Tree is strong and grounded into the earth.

Stand on one leg, bend the other knee and place the sole of your foot on your inner thigh.
Think of your standing leg as a tree trunk rooted into the ground and extend your arms out like tree branches.
Now try the other side!
Imagine it was windy would the branches of the tree move?

I am free like a bird

Pretend to be a Bird
A bird is carefree and loves to visit new places.

Stand on one leg, lift the other leg back up high, put one arm behind you and grab your ankle.
Place the other arm out in front of you.
Now try the other side!
Go outside today and count how many birds you can see...

Today is _____

(day of the week)

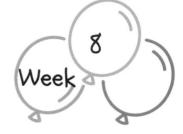

Week 8

The best part about today was

_____

_____

_____

_____

 A Picture of my day

This week includes two activities,
check out the next page!

Week 8

Circle of Friends

It was playtime in the school playground. Mark, Albert and Jack were best friends. They decided to play a game of football but quickly realised they needed more people to make a full team.

Mark noticed a boy playing all by himself in the distance so he said to Albert and Jack, "I know, lets ask that boy over there to join in our football game". Jack replied, "But he's not our friend". Then Albert said "That's okay. We can make new friends and he called him to join their game.

Then Jack saw a girl sitting by herself. She had no friends to play with because she was a new student at the school. The children asked her to join them too. The kids began to play together. Within a short time, all the kids in the playground had joined the game. They had a goalkeeper for each team and a referee.

The children had so much fun playing the game and the first round was a tie between the teams. Soon the bell rang and playtime was over. As the kids all laughed and chattered happily on their way back to class, they all realised that it was better playing altogether as they had so much fun and their circle of friends grew even bigger.

Week 9

THANK YOU
Letter

Dear _____

Thank you for

_____

_____

_____

_____

From: _____

XOXO

Give thanks to a parent, grandparent, friend, or teacher!
Give this letter to someone special

Mindful Sensory Game

Name 3 things you love that you can
See, Smell, Hear, Taste and Touch

See
_____
_____
_____

Smell
_____
_____
_____

Hear
_____
_____
_____

Taste
_____
_____
_____

Touch
_____
_____
_____

Family Fun Game

Week 11

1. Pick a letter

2. Think of something you are grateful for beginning with that letter

Example: I pick the letter 'B'

I AM GRATEFUL FOR MY WARM BED

This week includes two activities, check out the next page!

Bedtime Gratitude Blessing

The night sets in
Stars twinkle in the sky
We get ready to close our eyes
As the day has now passed by

We wash our face and brush our teeth
Getting ready for a nice long sleep
We snuggle into our warm bed
Thankful for the day ahead

Our minds drift back
To the fun we had today
How we laughed and played
And made friends along the way

So dream sweet dreams
And rest peacefully tonight
As tomorrow is a new day
Which will be full of delight

Night night x

P.s Hang this up in your room and say
it before bedtime!

Gratitude Yoga Poses

I am a bright like a star

Pretend to be like a Star
A star is bright and lights up the sky at night.

Lie on the ground and stretch your
arms and legs out like a star.
Remember you are a star and you brighten up
everyone you meet with your smile!

I am Calm like a Owl

Pretend to be like an Owl
An Owl is calm and wise.

Sit on the ground and cross your legs.
Lift your arms up and take a deep breath in and
when you exhale drop your arms down by your
side.
Remember it is easy to feel calm when you take a
big deep breath into your tummy.

 Play your favourite music!

This week includes two activities,
check out the next page!

Buddy Mirror Game

 **Step 1**   Stand facing your buddy

Pick one person to be the "mirror master"
The mirror master makes body movements and the other person must copy or "mirror" the movements.

Step 2

Jump, step, wiggle and bend!
Your buddy must try to "mirror" your movements.

 Try the yoga poses!

Step 3   After your buddy has copied you for a few minutes, let your buddy be the mirror master.

Tip: The mirror master can imagine he or she has magical superpowers.
🎵 Don't forget to play your favourite music!

Circle of Friends Activity

This week choose 4 people in your class you would like to know more about and fill in the boxes below!

Week 13

Kindness

Name:

_____

Favourite Food:

_____

Share

Name:

_____

Favourite Colour:

_____

Name:

_____

Their birthday is:

_____

Name:

_____

Favourite game:

_____

Include Everyone

Help Others

Random Acts of Kindness

Pick one activity to do every day this week!

Smile at everyone you meet!

 Donate toys & books to chairty

Share with others

 Bake cupcakes for someone special

Give flowers to your teacher

 hello

Say hello to everyone you know

Help make dinner

Feed the birds

Ask someone new at school to play

Say please & thank you

Tidy your bedroom

Hold the door open for someone

Gratitude Rocks

What you need?

Smooth flat Rocks from outside

Paint Brush

Your Buddy

Paint

Place your rocks/stones on some newspaper and paint them using your favourite colours.

 Write on the stones things you love or paint a picture.

Give the stone to someone you love

Family

Friends

Teacher

Write 3 things you love about school

1 _____

2 _____

3 _____

Write one thing you love to do in Spring/Summer/Autumn/Winter below...

Spring _____

Summer _____

Autumn _____

Winter _____

This week includes two activities, check out the next page!

Belly Balloon Breathing

This fun exercise helps you relax!

What is your favourite colour?
Imagine that your favourite coloured balloon is in your belly.
Place your hands on your belly.
Breathe in slowly through your nose and feel your belly get bigger like a balloon.

Now open your mouth and slowly blow all the air out letting your belly sink down flat as if letting down the imaginary balloon.

Repeat but next time close your mouth and practise breathing in and out through your nose as you feel your belly expanding and shrinking.

I feel
so light

This is
so cool

Mindful Colouring

What are your favourite colours?
Get crayons, markers, or colouring
pencils and colour in the picture below!

This week includes two activities,
check out the next page!

Draw + Colour a picture of you and your buddy on the swing below!

Name some things that you like about playing outside?

The best part about my week

* Do this activity at the end of the week

Week 18

_____

_____

_____

_____

A Picture of my week

This week includes two activities,
check out the next page!

Buddy Yoga Poses

We are Powerful

Stand beside your buddy
Begin by standing up tall
with your feet apart and your
arms by your side.
Take a big step back with one foot,
bend your front knee and lift your two
arms up and shout..
"WE ARE POWERFUL"

Play your favourite music

We are Brave

Stand opposite your buddy
Hold your buddy's hand
Lift one leg up behind you and
reach your arm back to hold
your leg.
Shout "WE ARE BRAVE"

Buddy Bubble Breath

This is such a really fun exercise to do with your buddy!

What you need?

plastic cup

Straw

Water

Buddy

Fill the cup 1/4 full with water
Get a straw each
Inhale deeply through your nose and breathe out slowly through the straw making bubbles into the glass.
Challenge your buddy...
See who can make the biggest bubbles without spilling any of the water!

Week 20

My Wish Jar

Make a WISH + draw it inside the magic jar!

I am thankful for...

Colour in all your favourite things that you are thankful for below. Think about why they make you happy.

Birds singing

Hugs & Kisses

My pet

My cosy bed

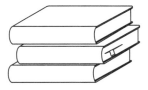

Butterflies

ME

Books to read

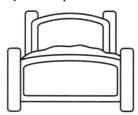

Bedtime stories

Ice-cream

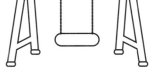

Playing outside

Week 21

My Word Search

Week 22

A B C D E F

G H I J K L

M N O P Q R

S T U V W

X Y Z

Circle and colour in the
letters of the words
' I AM THANKFUL '

John was on his way to see his aunt when he saw a blind man trying to cross the street. John walked up to the man and asked if he needed help.

"Yes, I'd appreciate it," the blind man said.

John helped him across the street. When he got to his aunt's house he realised that she wasn't at home. The weather had gotten cloudy and he had no umbrella with him. Soon, it began to rain and John was afraid of getting wet. Suddenly, the lady next door poked her head out of her window and called out to him.

"You can shelter with us until the rain stops," she said.

She was his aunt's friend and John had met her many times. She had a son around John's age too. The two little boys began to play. Then John heard a sound.

"What's that sound?" John asked.

"That's my dad's walking stick hitting the floor," the boy replied.

A blind man walked into the living room. It was the same man John helped earlier that day.

"I recognise that voice," the man said.

"Yes, I was the boy who helped you cross the street," John replied.

The blind man's wife thanked John and also asked him to stay for dinner. John had a wonderful time playing with his new friend. When John's aunt returned that evening, she was happy that John had shown so much kindness to the blind man.

What is your favourite pastime ?

_____

_____

_____

enjoy!   friends

Draw a picture of your favourite pastime

Week 25

I am thankful for...

On each love heart write something or
someone you are thankful for.
Cut hearts out. (To be done by an adult).
Put the hearts in your very own Gratitude Jar
from Week 26 activity!

My Gratitude Jar

Open Happiness

What you need:

Empty Jar & Lid

Paint

Glitter + Glue

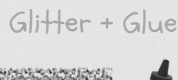 

How to make your own Gratitude jar?

Decorate the jar with paint and glitter.
Place the love hearts you made from Week 25
activity in the journal into the jar.

Tip: If you ever need cheering up, read some of the
love hearts in the jar and try and find something
that day to be grateful for to add to the jar!

This 26 week Gratitude Journal was created by two sisters Linda & Suzanne to help kids at a young age to identify and recognise all the things in their life (big and small) that they can be thankful for.

As adults we became interested in self-development & positive psychology. We quickly learned the huge benefits that a gratitude journal has on your overall level of happiness & wellbeing.

This inspired us to create this amazing gift for your child that helps build lifelong habits which begin in the early years of childhood development.

If you loved this product as much as we loved creating it, we would like to hear your feedback by leaving us a review on our Facebook page.

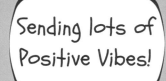

Sending lots of Positive Vibes!

 @positivevibes.ie   @positive_vibes.ie

Sharing is Caring

On the next page there is a really cool gift from us to you!

We know how good you are at sharing so we would kindly ask you to share 10 of your stickers with friends at school.